THE

Straub

BEER PARTY
DRINKS HANDBOOK

Rock the Straub's *

sb

ALSO BY JOHN E. SCHLIMM II

The Ultimate Elk Cookbook from the Heart of Elk Country
(with Steven K. Troha)

The Straub Beer Cookbook

Corresponding With History

THE

Straub

BEER PARTY
DRINKS HANDBOOK

---

150 DRINK RECIPES USING BEER

RECIPES SELECTED,
EDITED, & INTRODUCED BY

JOHN E. SCHLIMM II

Stohn Books
St. Marys, Pennsylvania

Copyright © 2004 By John E. Schlimm II

Cover Design Copyright © 2004
By John E. Schlimm II & Steven K. Troha

Produced & Published By
Stohn Books, Inc.
St. Marys, PA 15857

FIRST EDITION

ISBN 0-9752515-2-X
(#9632)

All rights reserved. No part of this book may be reproduced in
any form or by any electronic or mechanical means, including
information storage or retrieval systems, without written
permission from the publisher. For information, please address:
Stohn Books, Inc., 481 Brussells St., St. Marys, PA 15857

Please visit our web site at www.stohnbooks.com

Manufactured and Printed in the
United States of America

WARNING!

Some recipes in this book use fire and combustibles.
Extreme caution should be taken when using fire and
combustibles with these recipes. The publisher and
author are not responsible for any injuries that occur from
the use of fire and combustibles with these drinks. These
recipes are designed for adults of legal drinking age and
are not to be utilized by individuals under the legal
drinking age.

To

MY MOM,
GRANDMA SKOK, HELEN, & MIRIAM

Who taught me how to laugh
and the joy of always having
one last drink together

AND

CRAIG & JESS

Who taught me just how
fun drinking can be and to
the H. moment that was ours

ACKNOWLEDGMENTS

I would like to extend a special thanks to the following people, whose contributions through editorial support, advice, and encouragement were invaluable in writing this book: Patty Burden – my editorial and culinary consultant, Steven K. Troha – my most treasured editor, my parents – my most ardent supporters, Patty Brock & the Straub Brewery, Inc. Board of Directors – for their encouragement, Peter & Sabina Straub – my inspiration, and, as always, Straub Bear Run – my roots & my wings.

FROM THE BEGINNING OF TIME…

Beer has satisfied the thirsty, celebrated the victorious, and heralded rites of passage. It has traveled the globe from the taverns and pubs of the Old World to the clubs and mini-bars of the Modern Village. Whether in a mug or bottle or keg, beer stands alone as the preeminent party icon of tailgating, 21st birthdays, summer picnics, holiday gatherings, bachelor parties, and girls' nights out.

In *The Straub Beer Party Drinks Handbook*, beer lends its unique taste to the cause of the parched and thirsty once more, joining forces with the other big shots on the drink circuit. Throughout this collection of mixed drinks, chuggers, shots & shooters, chasers, party punches, floats & milkshakes, and flaming drinks, beer aims to please its fans with some of the world's most delicious thirst quenchers.

So gather your friends together, line-up those mugs and shot glasses, fill your ice bucket, place the measuring cups, measuring spoons, picks, and stirs on stand-by, and break out the Straubs and other favorite beers, vodka, gin, and the rest of the bar gang. Follow the recipes as you wish, adding a little more here or a little less there, a new dash of this or a new dash of that, and let the party begin…

Contents

"A woman drove me to drink and I didn't even have the decency to thank her."

W.C. Fields

Straub Beer
Mixed Drinks

SEVEN & STRAUBS

Ingredients:

10 ounces Straub Beer
2 ounces 7-Up
1/2 teaspoon lime juice
Crushed ice

Directions:

Combine all ingredients, stirring well.

Brewing Notes:

BUZZY
NAVEL

Ingredients:

1/3 ounce vodka
1/3 ounce peach schnapps
1/3 ounce Straub Beer
Orange juice

Directions:

Combine the vodka, peach schnapps, and Straub Beer on the rocks in a highball glass, stirring well. Fill the remainder of the glass with the orange juice.

Brewing Notes:

STRAUB BEER SNAKEBITE

Ingredients:

2 ounces Straub Beer
2 ounces apple cider
Dash of raspberry liqueur
Ice

Directions:

Combine all ingredients in a shaker, shaking well, and then pour into a glass.

Brewing Notes:

LEMON JACK STRAUBS

Ingredients:

1 ounce vodka
1 ounce Jack Daniel's Whiskey
1 ounce lemonade
1 ounce Straub Beer

Directions:

Combine all ingredients on the rocks, stirring well.

Brewing Notes:

STRAUB BEER JUNGLE JUICE

Ingredients:

1 1/2 ounces white rum
1 1/2 ounces gin
1 1/2 ounces vodka
1 ounce triple sec
1 1/2 ounces sour mix
1 teaspoon grenadine
1 teaspoon Straub Beer

Directions:

Layer the ingredients in the above order over the rocks.

Brewing Notes:

STRAUB BEER BUSTER

Ingredients:

2 ounces vodka
12 ounces Straub Beer
Dash of Tabasco sauce

Directions:

Combine all ingredients on the rocks, stirring well.

Brewing Notes:

DR.
STRAUBS

Ingredients:

1 ounce amaretto
1 ounce vodka
1 ounce Bacardi 151 Proof Rum
1 ounce Dr. Pepper
1 ounce Straub Beer

Directions:

Combine the amaretto, vodka, and rum on the rocks. Stir in the Dr. Pepper and Straub Beer.

Brewing Notes:

STRAUB'S
HOOLA JUICE

Ingredients:

Pineapple juice (frozen into ice cubes)
12 ounces Straub Beer
4 tablespoons crushed pineapple
Pineapple chunks
Cherries

Directions:

Place the pineapple ice cubes in a blender and crush.
Pour the crushed pineapple ice into a glass. Add the
Straub Beer, stirring well. Top with the crushed
pineapple. Garnish by alternating the pineapple chunks
and cherries on a pick and laying it across the top of the
glass.

Brewing Notes:

STRAUB BEER
ICED TEA

Ingredients:

4 ounces unsweetened iced tea
Sugar (to taste)
12 ounces Straub Beer
Lemon slice
Sprig of mint

Directions:

Combine the iced tea and sugar on the rocks. Add the
Straub Beer, stirring to mix and dissolve the sugar.
Garnish with the lemon slice and sprig of mint.

Brewing Notes:

MALIBU RUMBLE

Ingredients:

5 ounces Bacardi 151 Black Bat Rum
2 ounces blue curacao
2 ounces Malibu Rum
Splash of Straub Beer
Crushed ice
Mountain Dew

Directions:

Combine all ingredients, except the Mountain Dew, in a
tall glass, stirring well. Fill the remainder of the glass with
the Mountain Dew.

Brewing Notes:

STRAUB BEER SUNRISE

Ingredients:

12 ounces Straub Beer
1 ounce amaretto
1 ounce orange juice
Orange slice

Directions:

Combine all ingredients on the rocks, stirring well.
Garnish with the orange slice.

Brewing Notes:

STRAUB BEER BULLET

Ingredients:

2 ounces tequila
1 ounce Kahlua
1 ounce whiskey
1 ounce Straub Beer
1 ounce Mountain Dew

Directions:

Combine all ingredients, stirring well.

Brewing Notes:

ST. MARYS ROOT BEER

Ingredients:

1 ounce Galliano
1 ounce Kahlua
1 ounce cola
Crushed ice
2 1/2 ounces club soda
1 teaspoon Straub Beer

Directions:

In a shaker, combine the Galliano, Kahlua, cola, and crushed ice, shaking well. Strain into a glass and add the club soda and Straub Beer. Serve on the rocks.

Brewing Notes:

STRAUB-B-Q

Ingredients:

1 ounce Irish whiskey
2 ounces V-8 Juice
1 teaspoon barbecue sauce (smokey)
1 teaspoon lemon juice
Straub Beer
Celery stalk

Directions:

Combine all ingredients, except the Straub Beer, in a highball glass. Fill the remainder of the glass with the Straub Beer. Garnish with the celery.

Brewing Notes:

STRAUB BEER
RED-HEADED MARY

Ingredients:

8 ounces tomato juice
Splash of Tabasco sauce
Splash of Worcestershire sauce
4 ounces Straub Beer
Seasoned salt (to taste)
Pepper (to taste)
Celery stalk

Directions:

Layer the ingredients in the above order over the rocks, adding the seasoning to taste. Garnish with the celery.

Brewing Notes:

PEACH
FIZZ

Ingredients:

7 ounces peach schnapps
3 ounces Straub Beer
1 ounce Jack Daniel's Whiskey
3 ounces Slice
2 ounces lemonade
Ice

Directions:

Combine all ingredients in a shaker. Shake well and
strain into a glass.

Brewing Notes:

STRAUB BEER COUNTRY LEMONADE

Ingredients:

6 ounces gin
1 can lemonade concentrate
12 ounces Straub Beer
Water (optional & to taste)
Lemon slices

Directions:

Combine all ingredients on the rocks in a pitcher, stirring well. Garnish with the lemon slices.

Brewing Notes:

STRAUB BEER BLEEDER

Ingredients:

1/2 ounce vodka
1/2 ounce rum
1/2 ounce gin
1/2 ounce tequila
1/2 ounce triple sec
1/2 ounce brandy
1/2 ounce Malibu Rum
2 ounces Straub Beer
1/2 ounce lime juice
Splash of grenadine

Directions:

Combine all ingredients on the rocks, stirring well.

Brewing Notes:

BERRY SWEET STRAUBS

Ingredients:

1 1/2 cups strawberries
1 1/2 cups raspberries
1 1/2 cups blueberries
1 1/2 cups blackberries
2 lemons (squeezed)
Lemon juice
1/2 cup powdered sugar
Crushed ice
3 (12-ounce) bottles Straub Beer

Directions:

In a blender, combine all of the berries and reduce the
mixture to juice. Add the juice from the 2 lemons, mixing
well. Dip the rim of each frosted glass in the lemon juice
and then the sugar. Fill each glass halfway with the
crushed ice. Pour the berry-lemon juice mixture into the
glasses, covering the ice. Fill the remainder of each
glass with the Straub Beer.

Brewing Notes:

STRAUB BEER OVER CHERRY ROCKS

Ingredients:

Cherry 7-Up (frozen into ice cubes)
Cherries (frozen inside the ice cubes)
12 ounces Straub Beer
2 ounces Cherry 7-Up

Directions:

To make the cherry rocks, pour the Cherry 7-Up into an
ice tray. Place one cherry in each ice tray cube and
freeze. Fill a glass with the frozen cherry rocks and
combine the Straub Beer and 2 ounces of Cherry 7-Up,
stirring well.

Brewing Notes:

STRAUB BEER
GINGER ALE

Ingredients:

6 ounces Straub Beer
6 ounces ginger ale
Lemon slice
1 cherry

Directions:

Combine the Straub Beer and ginger ale in a frosted glass, stirring well. Garnish with the lemon slice and cherry.

Brewing Notes:

ABSOLUT VANILLA STRAUBS

Ingredients:

2 ounces Absolut Vanilla Vodka
12 ounces Straub Beer

Directions:

Combine both ingredients on the rocks, stirring well.

Brewing Notes:

SOUR
STRAUBS

Ingredients:

1/2 ounce fresh lime juice
1 cup Straub Beer
Lime slice

Directions:

Stir the lime juice into the Straub Beer. Garnish with the lime slice.

Brewing Notes:

STRAUB BEER
RUM IN THE DARK

Ingredients:

10 ounces Straub Beer
1 ounce dark rum

Directions:

Combine both ingredients on the rocks, stirring well.

Brewing Notes:

STRAUB BEER
DEW DROP

Ingredients:

3 ounces Straub Beer
2 ounces tequila
1 ounce Bacardi Dark Rum
1 ounce ouzo
Mountain Dew

Directions:

Combine all ingredients, except the Mountain Dew, in a
tall glass. Top with the Mountain Dew.

Brewing Notes:

THE BIG

O

Ingredients:

1 ounce curacao
Splash of orange juice
Ice
12 ounces Straub Beer

Directions:

Combine the curacao, orange juice, and ice in a shaker,
shaking well. Add the shaker mixture to the Straub Beer,
stirring well.

Brewing Notes:

STRAUB BEER
LEMON TICKLER

Ingredients:

1 ounce cynar
1/3 ounce lemon syrup
12 ounces Straub Beer

Directions:

Combine the cynar and lemon syrup in a frosted mug.
Add the Straub Beer, filling the mug and stirring well.

Brewing Notes:

DAREDEVIL'S BREW

Ingredients:

4 ounces gin
3 ounces Straub Beer
Ice

Directions:

Combine all ingredients in a shaker, shaking well. Strain
the liquid into a glass.

Brewing Notes:

STRAUB
HOUND DOG

Ingredients:

3 ounces vodka
12 ounces Straub Beer
4 ounces Southern Comfort

Directions:

Combine all ingredients on the rocks, stirring well.

Brewing Notes:

STRAUB BEER
TONGUE TINGLER

Ingredients:

2 ounces Everclear
2 ounces vodka
2 ounces gin
1 ounce dark rum
1 ounce peppermint schnapps
2 ounces Straub Beer
Cola

Directions:

Combine all ingredients, except the cola, on the rocks in a highball glass. Fill the remainder of the glass with the cola, stirring well.

Brewing Notes:

STRAUB BEER
GRIZZLY

Ingredients:

1/4 ounce triple sec
1/4 ounce rum
1/4 ounce vodka
1/4 ounce gin
1/4 ounce tequila
1/4 ounce bourbon
1/4 ounce scotch
12 ounces Straub Beer
12 ounces stout of choice

Directions:

Combine all ingredients, except the Straub Beer and
stout, in a mug, stirring well. Fill the remainder of the
mug with equal parts of the Straub Beer and stout.

Brewing Notes:

STRAUB
BEER MIST

Ingredients:

1 1/2 ounces Irish Mist
16 ounces Straub Beer

Directions:

Combine both ingredients, stirring well.

Brewing Notes:

SKIP & GO NAKED

Ingredients:

1 ounce gin
2 ounces sour mix
Straub Beer

Directions:

Stir together the gin and sour mix in a Collins glass filled
with ice. Fill the remainder of the glass with the Straub
Beer, stirring lightly.

Brewing Notes:

STRAUB BEER MIMOSA

Ingredients:

4 ounces Straub Beer
4 ounces orange juice
Splash of champagne

Directions:

Pour the Straub Beer into a champagne glass. Add the orange juice, stirring well. Top with the champagne.

Brewing Notes:

STRAUB
BLUE MOON

Ingredients:

1 ounce vodka
2 teaspoons blue curacao
Straub Beer

Directions:

Pour the vodka and blue curacao into a Pilsner glass. Fill
the remainder of the glass with the Straub Beer. Stir
gently.

Brewing Notes:

STRAUB BEER
FIRE & ICE

Ingredients:

5 ounces vodka
1 1/2 ounces Fire and Ice
1/4 cup Straub Beer
1/2 cup cola

Directions:

Combine all ingredients on the rocks, stirring well.

Brewing Notes:

THE
O. P.

Ingredients:

1 ounce Malibu Rum
1 ounce peach schnapps
Orange juice
Pineapple juice
1 teaspoon Straub Beer
Pineapple chunks
Cherries
Orange slice

Directions:

Combine the rum and peach schnapps in a shaker, shaking well. Strain the mixture into a Collins glass filled with crushed ice. Pour in equal amounts of each juice. Top with the Straub Beer. Garnish by alternating the pineapple chunks and cherries on a pick and placing it along with the orange slice on the side of the glass.

Brewing Notes:

STRAUB BEER SOUTHERN JACK

Ingredients:

1 cup Southern Comfort
1 cup Jack Daniel's Whiskey
16 ounces Straub Beer

Directions:

Combine all ingredients on the rocks, stirring well.

Brewing Notes:

STRAUB BEER CINNER

Ingredients:

2 parts cinnamon schnapps (chilled)
1 part Straub Beer
Splash of grenadine
Cinnamon stick

Directions:

Pour the cinnamon schnapps into a glass followed by the Straub Beer on the rocks. Top with the grenadine and add the cinnamon stick as a stir.

Brewing Notes:

STRAUB BEER
EEKING MONKEY

Ingredients:

3 shots 151 proof rum
4 shots spiced rum
1 ounce lime juice
1 ounce lemon juice
1 ounce papaya juice
2 ounces orange juice
3 ounces coconut milk
Crushed ice
4 ounces Straub Beer
Shredded coconut
Papaya chunks
Lime slice
Lemon slice

Directions:

Combine the rum and spiced rum in a shaker, shaking
well. Stir in the juices, coconut milk, and ice, shaking
well. Add the mixture to the Straub Beer, stirring well.
Top with the shredded coconut. Garnish with the papaya
chunks on a pick and place the lime and lemon slices on
the side of the glass.

Brewing Notes:

STRAUB BEERTINI

Ingredients:

3 parts dry vermouth
3 parts sweet vermouth
3 parts gin
3 parts whiskey
8 parts Straub Beer
1 drop blue curacao
1 drop red vodka

Directions:

Combine the vermouths, gin, and whiskey on the rocks in a martini glass. Add the Straub Beer followed by the blue curacao and red vodka.

Brewing Notes:

STRAUB BEER JAMMER

Ingredients:

1 shot rum
12 ounces Straub Beer
2 tablespoons lime juice

Directions:

Add the rum to the Straub Beer in a frosted glass. Add the lime juice, stirring well.

Brewing Notes:

STRAUB BEER
HANGOVER

Ingredients:

2 ounces vodka
3 ounces Straub Beer
4 ounces tomato juice
Salt (to taste)
Seasoned salt (to taste)
Celery stalk

Directions:

Combine all ingredients, stirring well. Garnish with the
celery.

Brewing Notes:

LOVE POTION #7

Ingredients:

Splash of grenadine
2/3 glass Straub Beer
1/3 glass 7-Up

Directions:

Add each ingredient to a glass in the above order over the rocks, stirring well.

Brewing Notes:

SOUR MOMMA

Ingredients:

1 ounce gin
1 ounce vodka
1 ounce grenadine
1 ounce sour mix
Straub Beer

Directions:

Combine the gin, vodka, grenadine, and sour mix in a shaker, shaking well. Pour the mixture into a Collins glass filled with ice, filling about 1/2 to 3/4 of the glass. Fill the remainder of the glass with the Straub Beer.

Brewing Notes:

STRAUB BEER BENDER

Ingredients:

1 shot vodka
1/2 shot gin
2 ounces Gatorade
4 ounces Crown Royal
1 teaspoon salt
Splash of lemon juice
6 ounces Straub Beer

Directions:

Combine all ingredients on the rocks, stirring well.

Brewing Notes:

STRAUB BEER CRUSH

Ingredients:

12 ounces whiskey
12 ounces Straub Beer
12 ounces frozen lemonade concentrate
1 cup crushed ice
Lemon slices

Directions:

Combine all ingredients in a blender, blending well.
Garnish each glass with a lemon slice.

Brewing Notes:

STRAUB BEER SOUR PUSS

Ingredients:

1 1/2 ounces amaretto
1 teaspoon Straub Beer
3 ounces sour mix
Splash of Sprite

Directions:

Combine the amaretto, Straub Beer, and sour mix in a glass filled with ice. Top with the Sprite, stirring well.

Brewing Notes:

STRAUB BEER
GRAND DAME

Ingredients:

1/2 ounce vodka
1/2 ounce gin
1/2 ounce rum
1/2 ounce Grand Marnier
1/4 ounce Tia Maria
1/4 ounce Kahlua
1 ounce sour mix
Splash of cranberry juice
Crushed ice
Straub Beer draft foam

Directions:

Combine all of the alcohol, except the Straub Beer draft foam. Add the sour mix. Add the cranberry juice and crushed ice, stirring well. Top with the foam from the Straub Beer draft.

Brewing Notes:

STRAUB BEER
TWIST & SHOUT

Ingredients:

1 ounce vodka
2 ounces lemon soda
Straub Beer (to taste)
Cola (to taste)

Directions:

Combine the vodka and lemon soda, filling 1/2 of a
frosted glass. Add the Straub Beer and cola as desired.

Brewing Notes:

CRANBERRY STRAUBS

Ingredients:

12 ounces Straub Beer
1 ounce cranberry juice

Directions:

Combine both ingredients on the rocks, stirring well.

Brewing Notes:

AFTER DINNER MINT

Ingredients:

1/3 part cognac
1/3 part crème de menthe
1/3 part Straub Beer
Ice (add green food coloring when making the ice)

Directions:

Combine all ingredients in a shaker, shaking well, and
then pour into a glass.

Brewing Notes:

THE ORIGINAL STRAUB BEER MARGARITA

Ingredients:

1 pitcher ice
12 ounces frozen limeade concentrate
12 ounces Straub Beer
12 ounces tequila
3 splashes margarita mix
1/4 cup salt
Lime slices

Directions:

Pour the ice into a blender until it is 3/4 full. Add the limeade, Straub Beer, and tequila, blending until smooth. Add the margarita mix. Salt the rims of the margarita glasses. Pour the mixture into the glasses and garnish with the lime slices.

Brewing Notes:

STRAUB BEER
RED, WHITE, & BLUE

Ingredients:

6 ounces Straub Beer
1/2 ounce blueberry brandy
2 ounces peach schnapps
1 ounce vodka
1/2 ounce Everclear
Crushed ice

Directions:

Combine all ingredients, stirring well.

Brewing Notes:

STRAUB BEER
APPLE TREE CIDER

Ingredients:

8 ounces Straub Beer
8 ounces apple cider

Directions:

Combine both ingredients, stirring well.

Brewing Notes:

STRAUB BEER VOLCANO

Ingredients:

2 parts Straub Beer
2 parts coconut rum
1 part vodka
1 part triple sec
2 parts melon liqueur

Directions:

Combine all ingredients on the rocks, stirring well.

Brewing Notes:

STRAUB BEER
GYPSY

Ingredients:

2 parts Jagermeister
1 part gin
1 1/2 parts Drambuie
1 part Baileys Irish Cream
Straub Beer
Crème de menthe

Directions:

Combine the Jagermeister, gin, Drambuie, and Baileys
Irish Cream on the rocks. Top with equal amounts of the
Straub Beer and crème de menthe.

Brewing Notes:

STRAUB BEER SCREWDRIVER

Ingredients:

2 ounces vodka
8 ounces orange juice
12 ounces Straub Beer

Directions:

Combine the vodka and orange juice on the rocks, stirring well. Stir in the Straub Beer.

Brewing Notes:

GOODNIGHT, SWEETHEART

Ingredients:

1 gallon Straub Beer
8 ounces honey
Pepper

Directions:

In a saucepan, combine the Straub Beer and honey,
stirring and heating the mixture until the honey is
dissolved. Place the pepper in an infuser and steep it in
the mixture overnight. Serve the drink hot in mugs.

Brewing Notes:

STRAUB BEER CREAMY SODA

Ingredients:

1 part Straub Beer
1 part cream soda

Directions:

Combine both ingredients on the rocks, stirring well.

Brewing Notes:

STRAUB BEER CHULITRO

Ingredients:

1 1/2 ounces pisco
2 ice cubes
Cola (to fill the glass)
Dash of Straub Beer
Lemon juice (to taste)

Directions:

Layer the ingredients in the above order.

Brewing Notes:

STRAUBERRY DAIQUIRI

Ingredients:

1/2 cup ice
5 ounces Straub Beer
1/2 ounce tequila
1/2 ounce light rum
3 ounces strawberry daiquiri mix
3 ounces margarita mix
Fresh strawberries

Directions:

Pour the ingredients (including some of the fresh
strawberries) into a blender in the above order, blending
until frothy. Garnish with the fresh strawberries on a pick.

Brewing Notes:

STRAUB BEER
TEQUILA SUNRISE

Ingredients:

4 ounces tequila
1 ounce rum
1 ounce vodka
8 ounces Straub Beer

Directions:

Pour 2 ounces of the tequila over ice into a shaker and shake. Add the rum and vodka, and shake. Add this mixture to the Straub Beer. Add the rest of the tequila, pouring it over the back of a spoon.

Brewing Notes:

BORDER CROSSING

Ingredients:

2 ounces tequila
Dash of bitters
Straub Beer

Directions:

Combine the tequila and bitters in a highball glass,
stirring well. Fill the remainder of the glass with the
Straub Beer.

Brewing Notes:

STRAUB BIERE

Ingredients:

1 ounce Amer Picon
1/3 ounce lemon syrup
Straub Beer

Directions:

Combine the Amer Picon and lemon syrup in a mug. Fill the remainder of the mug with the Straub Beer, stirring well.

Brewing Notes:

CLAM'S EYE

Ingredients:

Pinch of salt
Dash of lemon juice
Pinch of pepper
6 ounces clamato juice
6 ounces Straub Beer
1 ounce Tabasco sauce (or to taste)

Directions:

Combine the salt, lemon juice, and pepper. Add the
clamato juice. Slowly add the Straub Beer. Add the
Tabasco sauce. Serve on the rocks.

Brewing Notes:

STRAUB BEER DREAMSICLE

Ingredients:

1 ounce amaretto
4 ounces Straub Beer
4 ounces orange juice
2 drops sugar syrup
Crushed ice

Directions:

Combine all ingredients, stirring well.

Brewing Notes:

HEAD
TRIP

Ingredients:

1 ounce Everclear
2 tablespoons Straub Beer
2 ounces butterscotch schnapps
Root beer (to taste)

Directions:

Combine all ingredients on the rocks, stirring well.

Brewing Notes:

"The problem with the world is that everyone is a few drinks behind."

Humphrey Bogart

Straub Beer
Chuggers

STRAUB BEER
BOILERMAKER

Ingredients:

2 ounces whiskey
10 ounces Straub Beer

Directions:

Pour the whiskey into a shot glass and the Straub Beer
into a mug. Drop the shot glass into the mug and chug.

Brewing Notes:

STRAUB BEER
WIDOWMAKER

Ingredients:

1 ounce vodka
16 ounces Straub Beer

Directions:

Pour the vodka into a shot glass and the Straub Beer into
a mug. Drop the shot glass into the mug and chug.

Brewing Notes:

KAHLUA
SHOOT OUT

Ingredients:

1 ounce Kahlua
12 ounces Straub Beer

Directions:

Pour the Kahlua into a shot glass and the Straub Beer
into a mug. Drop the shot glass into the mug and chug.

Brewing Notes:

STRAUB BEER
DEPTH CHARGE

Ingredients:

1 ounce Drambuie
12 ounces Straub Beer

Directions:

Pour the Drambuie into a shot glass and the Straub Beer
into a mug. Drop the shot glass into the mug and chug.

Brewing Notes:

STRAUB BEER SAMBUCA

Ingredients:

1 ounce sambuca
12 ounces Straub Beer

Directions:

Pour the sambuca into a shot glass and the Straub Beer
into a mug. Drop the shot glass into the mug and chug.

Brewing Notes:

WOODPECKER

Ingredients:

10 ounces Mountain Dew
2 ounces vodka
12 ounces Straub Beer
Dash of honey

Directions:

Combine all ingredients, stirring well. Chug.

Brewing Notes:

TEQUILA
SKY ROCKET

Ingredients:

1 ounce tequila
12 ounces Straub Beer
1 lime

Directions:

Pour the tequila into a shot glass and the Straub Beer into a mug. Drop the shot glass into the mug, squeeze the lime on top, and chug.

Brewing Notes:

BEER BEER CHUGGER

Ingredients:

1 ounce root beer schnapps
8 ounces Straub Beer

Directions:

Pour the root beer schnapps into a shot glass and the Straub Beer into a mug. Drop the shot glass into the mug and chug.

Brewing Notes:

THE
MOULIN SLIDER

Ingredients:

1/2 ounce absinthe
1/2 ounce cinnamon schnapps
12 ounces Straub Beer

Directions:

Pour the absinthe and cinnamon schnapps into a shot
glass and the Straub Beer into a mug. Drink a quarter of
the Straub Beer, drop the shot glass into the mug, and
chug.

Brewing Notes:

STRAUB BEER
DANCIN' MOMMA

Ingredients:

1/2 ounce dark rum
1/2 ounce tequila
6 ounces Straub Beer

Directions:

Pour the dark rum and tequila into a shot glass, stirring
well. Pour the Straub Beer into a mug. Drop the shot
glass into the mug and chug.

Brewing Notes:

STRAUB BEER
LUNCH BOX

Ingredients:

1/2 ounce amaretto
4 ounces Straub Beer
1/2 ounce orange juice

Directions:

Pour the amaretto into a shot glass. Pour the Straub
Beer and orange juice into a mug, stirring well. Drop the
shot glass into the mug and chug.

Brewing Notes:

REBEL
WITH A STRAUBS

Ingredients:

3/4 ounce Rebel Yell 101
Bacardi Limon
6 ounces Straub Beer
Splash of cola

Directions:

Pour the Rebel Yell 101 into a shot glass and then fill the
rest of the shot glass with the Bacardi Limon. Pour the
Straub Beer into a mug, filling the mug halfway, and add
the cola. Drop the shot glass into the mug and chug.

Brewing Notes:

STRAUB BEER
HOT SAKE BOMB

Ingredients:

1 ounce hot sake
6 ounces Straub Beer

Directions:

Pour the sake into a shot glass and the Straub Beer into
a mug. Drop the shot glass into the mug and chug.

Brewing Notes:

STRAUBERRY JOLT

Ingredients:

1 1/2 ounces strawberry liqueur
12 ounces Straub Beer

Directions:

Pour the strawberry liqueur into a shot glass and the
Straub Beer into a mug. Drop the shot glass into the mug
and chug.

Brewing Notes:

STRAUB BEER BUCKSHOT

Ingredients:

1 ounce Midori
1/2 glass Straub Beer
1/2 glass 7-Up

Directions:

Pour the Midori into a shot glass. Pour the Straub Beer
into a mug followed by the 7-Up. Drop the shot glass into
the mug and chug.

Brewing Notes:

GREEN GOBLIN

Ingredients:

1 part gin
1 part sweet vermouth
1 part lime juice
1 part melon liqueur
16 ounces Straub Beer

Directions:

Pour all ingredients, except the Straub Beer, into a shot glass. Pour the Straub Beer into a mug. Drop the shot glass into the mug and chug.

Brewing Notes:

HUNTING CAMP SPECIAL

Ingredients:

1 shot 151 proof rum
1 shot tequila
1 shot bourbon
1 shot vodka
2 shots Wild Turkey
6 ounces Straub Beer

Directions:

Combine all ingredients, stirring well. Chug.

Brewing Notes:

VODKA CHUGGER

Ingredients:

3 ounces Straub Beer
1 1/2 ounces vodka
Dash of grenadine

Directions:

Combine all ingredients, stirring well. Chug.

Brewing Notes:

STRAUB BEER
IRISH CAR BOMB

Ingredients:

3/4 ounce Irish whiskey
3/4 ounce Irish cream
6 ounces Straub Beer

Directions:

Pour the whiskey and Irish cream into a shot glass and the Straub Beer into a mug. Drop the shot glass into the mug and chug.

Brewing Notes:

STRAUB BEER BLITZ

Ingredients:

1/3 ounce amaretto
2/3 ounce root beer schnapps
12 ounces Straub Beer

Directions:

Pour the amaretto and root beer schnapps into a shot glass and the Straub Beer into a mug. Drop the shot glass into the mug and chug.

Brewing Notes:

"I feel sorry for people who don't drink. When they wake up in the morning, that's as good as they're going to feel all day."

Frank Sinatra

Straub Beer
Shots & Shooters

STRAUB BEER TROPICAL NECTAR

Ingredients:

1/3 ounce Midori
1/6 ounce Straub Beer
1/3 ounce pineapple juice
1/5 ounce lemonade
Orange juice (to taste)

Directions:

Combine all ingredients in a shot glass, stirring well.

Brewing Notes:

STRAUB BEER
GIN BLAST

Ingredients:

1 ounce gin
1/2 ounce Straub Beer

Directions:

Combine both ingredients in a shot glass, stirring well.

Brewing Notes:

STRAUBUIE

Ingredients:

4 parts Drambuie
2 parts vodka
2 parts Straub Beer

Directions:

Combine all ingredients in a shot glass, stirring well.

Brewing Notes:

IRISH SETTER

Ingredients:

1/4 shot vodka
1/2 shot Baileys Irish Cream
Splash of Straub Beer

Directions:

Layer the vodka and Baileys Irish Cream in a shot glass.
Top with the Straub Beer.

Brewing Notes:

ATOMIC DIVA

Ingredients:

17 ounces aquavit
7 ounces Straub Beer

Directions:

Combine the Straub Beer and aquavit in a pitcher, stirring
well. Serve as shots.

Brewing Notes:

STRAUB BEER HONEY DROP

Ingredients:

2 parts tequila
1 part Straub Beer
Juice from 1 lime
1/2 teaspoon honey

Directions:

Combine the tequila, Straub Beer, and lime juice in a shot glass, mixing well. Pour the honey in a teaspoon. Drop the teaspoon of honey into the shot glass and drink quickly.

Brewing Notes:

"Always do sober what you said you'd do drunk. That will teach you to keep your mouth shut."

Ernest Hemingway

Straub Beer
Chasers

STRAUB BEER
NIGHT CRAWLER

Ingredients:

1/2 ounce tequila
1/2 ounce triple sec
1/2 ounce Jack Daniel's Whiskey
8 ounces Straub Beer

Directions:

Combine the tequila, triple sec, and whiskey in a shot glass. Down the shot and chase it with the Straub Beer.

Brewing Notes:

STRAUB BEER
PICKLED VODKA

Ingredients:

1 ounce vodka
1/2 ounce pickle juice of choice
8 ounces Straub Beer

Directions:

Combine the vodka and pickle juice in a shot glass,
stirring well. Down the shot and chase it with the Straub
Beer.

Brewing Notes:

WILD
TURKEY CHASE

Ingredients:

1 ounce Bacardi 151 Proof Rum
1 ounce Wild Turkey
8 ounces Straub Beer

Directions:

Combine the rum and Wild Turkey in a shot glass, stirring
well. Down the shot and chase it with the Straub Beer.

Brewing Notes:

STRAUB BEER
HOOT & HOLLER

Ingredients:

1/2 ounce triple sec
1/2 ounce Kahlua
1/2 ounce tequila
Ice
6 ounces Straub Beer

Directions:

Combine the triple sec, Kahlua, tequila, and ice in a
shaker, shaking well. Strain the mixture into a shot glass.
Down the shot and chase it with the Straub Beer.

Brewing Notes:

STRAUB'S
SHOOTING STARS

Ingredients:

1 ounce Jagermeister
1 ounce Jack Daniel's Whiskey
1 ounce Everclear
1 ounce After Shock
8 ounces Straub Beer

Directions:

Pour each of the 1 ounce drinks into a separate shot
glass. Down each shot separately in the order above and
chase them with the Straub Beer.

Brewing Notes:

DRUNKEN LEPRECHAUN

Ingredients:

1/3 ounce Baileys Irish Cream
2/3 ounce crème de menthe
1 ounce Straub Beer

Directions:

Combine the Baileys Irish Cream and crème de menthe
in a shot glass, stirring well. Down the shot and chase it
with the Straub Beer.

Brewing Notes:

STRAUB BEER
HOT BALLERS

Ingredients:

20 drops Tabasco sauce
1 shot tequila
1 shot peppermint schnapps
8 ounces Straub Beer

Directions:

Pour the Tabasco sauce, tequila, and peppermint schnapps into 3 different shot glasses. Down each shot separately in the order above and chase them with the Straub Beer.

Brewing Notes:

BEER
BALL HOOTER

Ingredients:

1 part tequila
1 part peppermint schnapps
Ice
8 ounces Straub Beer

Directions:

Combine the tequila, peppermint schnapps, and ice in a shaker, shaking well. Strain the mixture into a shot glass. Down the shot and chase it with the Straub Beer.

Brewing Notes:

STRAUB BEER BABBLER

Ingredients:

1/2 ounce amaretto
1/2 ounce Southern Comfort
8 ounces Straub Beer

Directions:

Combine the amaretto and Southern Comfort in a shot glass. Down the shot and chase it with the Straub Beer.

Brewing Notes:

REGGIE
ORIGINAL

Ingredients:

1 shot whiskey
8 ounces Straub Beer

Directions:

Down the shot and chase it with the Straub Beer.

Brewing Notes:

"Always remember that I have taken more out of alcohol than alcohol has taken out of me."

Winston Churchill

Straub Beer
Party Punches

STRAUB BEER CITRUS SUNSATION PUNCH

Ingredients:

2 cups sugar
2 cups water
6 lemons (juiced with the peels sliced)
1 cup orange juice
24 ounces Straub Beer
7-Up (frozen into ice cubes)
Orange slices

Directions:

Combine the sugar and water. Bring to a boil. Add the
lemon peels, remove from heat, and cover for 5 minutes.
Remove the peels. Add the lemon and orange juices.
Stir well. Pour into a pitcher and refrigerate for several
hours. Stir in the Straub Beer and 7-Up ice cubes just
before serving the punch. Garnish with the orange slices.

Brewing Notes:

STRAUB
BEER-TANG

Ingredients:

10 ounces Straub Beer
12 ounces orange juice
1 quart ginger ale
2 tablespoons lime juice
3 ounces sugar
Lemonade (frozen into ice cubes)

Directions:

Combine all ingredients, stirring well.

Brewing Notes:

STRAUB BEER
PINK PUNCH BUG

Ingredients:

1 can pink lemonade concentrate
12 ounces water
12 ounces vodka
12 ounces Straub Beer
Pink lemonade (frozen into ice cubes)

Directions:

Pour the lemonade into a gallon pitcher. Add the water
and vodka. Stir well. Add the Straub Beer and pink
lemonade ice cubes. Mix well.

Brewing Notes:

STRAUB BEER
GINGER PUNCH

Ingredients:

1 1/2 ounces gin
12 ounces Straub Beer
12 ounces ginger beer
Juice from 1/2 lemon
Splash of soda water
Ginger ale (frozen into ice cubes)

Directions:

Combine all ingredients, stirring well.

Brewing Notes:

STRAUB BEER
NEW YEAR'S PUNCH

Ingredients:

1 gallon vodka
1 gallon + 16 ounces Straub Beer
2 liters Sprite
1 can powdered lemonade mix
Sprite (frozen into ice cubes)
Cherries (frozen inside the ice cubes)
Orange rinds (frozen inside the ice cubes)
Green grapes (frozen inside the ice cubes)

Directions:

Combine all ingredients, stirring well.

Brewing Notes:

TOM & JERRY
BEER PUNCH

Ingredients:

24 ounces Straub Beer
1/2 cup sugar
1 cinnamon stick
1/4 teaspoon nutmeg
4 eggs
1/4 cup rum
1/4 cup brandy
1 teaspoon pure vanilla

Directions:

Combine the Straub Beer, sugar, cinnamon stick, and nutmeg. Heat the mixture until the sugar dissolves. Lightly beat the eggs while slowly adding the rum and brandy. Remove the Straub Beer mixture from the heat and remove the cinnamon stick. Stir in the egg mixture followed by the vanilla. Serve hot.

Brewing Notes:

SOUR PATCH PUNCH

Ingredients:

1 cup sugar
1 cup water
3 lemons (juiced with the zest removed and saved)
1/2 cup chilled grapefruit juice
12 ounces Straub Beer
Squirt (frozen into ice cubes)
Several lemon slices
Several cherries

Directions:

Combine the sugar and water and bring to a boil over a high heat. Stir until the sugar is dissolved. Add the lemon zest and remove the mixture from the heat. Cover and let cool for 10 minutes. Remove the lemon zest and allow the mixture to cool to room temperature. Add the lemon and grapefruit juices to the sugar mixture. Chill for 2 to 3 hours. Stir in the Straub Beer and Squirt ice cubes before serving. Garnish the servings with the lemon slices and cherries.

Brewing Notes:

STRAUB BEER
LEMON PUNCH

Ingredients:

1 can lemonade concentrate
36 ounces water
Lemonade (frozen into ice cubes)
24 ounces Straub Beer
1 1/2 cups rum
Lemon slices
Cherries
Sprigs of mint

Directions:

Combine the lemonade and water, stirring well. Pour the lemonade into a punch bowl filled with the lemonade ice cubes. Add the Straub Beer and rum, stirring well. Garnish with the lemon slices, cherries, and sprigs of mint.

Brewing Notes:

4ᵀᴴ OF JULY
PARADE PUNCH

Ingredients:

1 gallon vodka
2 quarts Straub Beer
4 cans lemonade concentrate
4 cups water
2 quarts fruit punch
Blueberry Kool-Aid (frozen into a star-shaped ice mold)
Fresh blueberries (frozen inside the ice mold)

Directions:

Combine all ingredients, except the ice mold, stirring well.
Pour the punch into a punch bowl and add the star-shaped blueberry ice mold.

Brewing Notes:

STRAUB
VINEYARD PUNCH

Ingredients:

1 quart vodka
1/2 gallon red wine
1 quart ginger ale
12 ounces Straub Beer
Ginger ale (frozen into ice cubes)
Red grapes (frozen inside the ice cubes)

Directions:

Combine all ingredients, except the Straub Beer and
ginger ale ice, stirring well. Add the Straub Beer. Add
the ginger ale ice. Stir well.

Brewing Notes:

FREEDOM
PUNCH

Ingredients:

1 fifth vodka
2 quarts + 8 ounces Straub Beer
2 scoops powdered lemonade
Water (to taste)
Sugar (to taste)
Ice
Raspberries (frozen inside the ice cubes)
Lemon slices

Directions:

Combine all ingredients, except the lemon slices, stirring well. Garnish with the lemon slices.

Brewing Notes:

STRAUB BEER ORIGINAL FRUIT PUNCH

Ingredients:

1 2/3 cups rum
12 ounces Straub Beer
4 cups orange juice
3 cups pineapple juice
2 cups Ocean Spray Juice
Splash of banana liqueur
Ice
Pineapple chunks
Banana slices
Cherries
Papaya chunks
Orange slices

Directions:

Combine all ingredients, except the fruit, stirring well.
Add all of the fruit, allowing it to float in the punch bowl.

Brewing Notes:

CLOUD 9

Ingredients:

1 quart vodka
1 quart brandy
1 quart gin
1 quart light rum
1 quart Lambrusco
3 gallons fruit punch
Ice
2 quarts + 8 ounces Straub Beer

Directions:

Combine all ingredients, adding the Straub Beer last
and stirring well.

Brewing Notes:

FALLEN APPLE PUNCH

Ingredients:

1/4 cup butter
1 cup sugar
1/2 teaspoon nutmeg
1/2 teaspoon ginger
8 apples (sliced)
2 quarts Straub Beer

Directions:

Melt the butter. Add the sugar, stirring well. Add the
nutmeg and ginger, continuing to stir. Place the apple
slices in the mixture. Top with the Straub Beer. Slowly
heat and serve warm.

Brewing Notes:

STRAUB BERRY PICKING PUNCH

Ingredients:

1 fifth vodka
3 (12-ounce) bottles Straub Beer
2 cans fruit punch
Ice (create using an ice mold)
Strawberries (frozen inside the ice mold)
Blueberries (frozen inside the ice mold)
Blackberries (frozen inside the ice mold)
Raspberries (frozen inside the ice mold)
3 lemons (sliced)
3 limes (sliced)

Directions:

Combine the vodka, Straub Beer, fruit punch, and ice mold. Garnish with the fruit slices. The berries may also be used to garnish the punch.

Brewing Notes:

MIDNIGHT MOON &
FIDDLE PUNCH

Ingredients:

16 ounces 151 proof rum
16 ounces blackberry brandy
12 ounces Straub Beer
1 can cola
1 can orange soda
1 can 7-Up
32 ounces pineapple juice
Ice

Directions:

Combine all ingredients, stirring well.

Brewing Notes:

BEACH PARTY PUNCH

Ingredients:

4 ounces rum
4 ounces vodka
4 ounces amaretto
4 ounces gin
24 ounces Straub Beer
1 can Sprite
8 ounces orange juice
8 ounces pineapple juice
Ice

Directions:

Combine all ingredients, stirring well.

Brewing Notes:

STRAUB BEER
WEDDING PUNCH

Ingredients:

7 cups vodka
7 cups gin
7 cups rum
13 1/2 quarts Straub Beer
10 quarts pink lemonade
Pink lemonade (frozen into ice cubes)

Directions:

Combine all ingredients, stirring well.

Brewing Notes:

ORANGE FIZZ

Ingredients:

8 ounces gin
11 ounces Straub Beer
16 ounces orange soda
Ice
Orange slices

Directions:

Combine all ingredients, except the orange slices in a
blender. Blend for 3 minutes. Garnish each serving with
an orange slice.

Brewing Notes:

MALIBU RUM RUN

Ingredients:

12 ounces Straub Beer
2 1/2 ounces Malibu Rum
1 1/2 cups orange juice
7 ounces 7-Up
2 splashes of lemon juice
9 ounces Straub Beer
6 ounces Mountain Dew
1 ounce Malibu Rum
Orange juice (frozen into an ice mold)
Lemon slices

Directions:

Combine the 12 ounces of Straub Beer, 2 1/2 ounces of
rum, orange juice, 7-Up, and lemon juice, stirring well.
Combine the 9 ounces of Straub Beer, Mountain Dew,
and 1 ounce of rum, stirring well. Combine both mixtures,
stirring well. Pour the punch into a punch bowl filled with
the orange juice ice mold. Garnish each glass with a
lemon slice.

Brewing Notes:

STRAUB BEER POLKA PUNCH

Ingredients:

Crushed ice
12 ounces Straub Beer
2 ounces vodka
2 ounces Southern Comfort
2 ounces sloe gin
2 ounces gin
2 ounces grenadine
7-Up
Orange juice

Directions:

Put a layer of crushed ice at the bottom of a pitcher. Add
the Straub Beer followed by the other ingredients. Top
off the remainder of the pitcher with equal amounts of
7-Up and orange juice. Stir well.

Brewing Notes:

STRAUB BEER PEACHY PUNCH

Ingredients:

2 cups vodka
12 ounces peach schnapps
36 ounces Straub Beer
1 quart water
1 package Orange Tang
Ice

Directions:

Combine all ingredients, stirring well.

Brewing Notes:

FRIENDSHIP PUNCH

Ingredients:

40 ounces Straub Beer
12 ounces ginger ale
1/4 shot vodka
1/4 shot light rum
1/2 shot amaretto
Ice

Directions:

Combine all ingredients, stirring well.

Brewing Notes:

SUN-KISSED PUNCH

Ingredients:

1 quart + 8 ounces Straub Beer
34 ounces vodka
2 gallons orange juice
Orange juice (frozen into an ice mold and crushed)

Directions:

Combine all ingredients, stirring well.

Brewing Notes:

STRAUB BEER POWER PUNCH

Ingredients:

12 (12-ounce) bottles Straub Beer
2 cans pink lemonade concentrate
13 ounces Absolut Vodka
13 ounces Canadian whisky
Pink lemonade (frozen into ice cubes)

Directions:

Combine all ingredients, stirring well.

Brewing Notes:

TRICK OR TREAT PUNCH

Ingredients:

1 gallon After Shock
11 ounces Straub Beer
12 ounces Jack Daniel's Orange Whiskey
10 ounces sparkling wine
3 ounces 7-Up
1/2 ounce apple juice
1 can Dr. Pepper
4 ounces grenadine
Dr. Pepper (frozen into ice cubes)
Gummy worms
Candy corn
Jolly Ranchers

Directions:

Combine all ingredients, except the candy, stirring well.
Garnish with the gummy worms, candy corn, Jolly
Ranchers, and any other candy of choice. Serve in a
punch bowl placed in a large hollowed-out pumpkin or a
plastic pumpkin.

Brewing Notes:

STRAUB'S HOLIDAY EGG NOG

Ingredients:

3 eggs (separated)
1/2 cup sugar
2 cups milk
OR
1 gallon prepared egg nog

12 ounces Straub Beer
1/4 cup brandy or bourbon
1 cup whipped cream
Nutmeg

Directions:

Beat the egg yolks with 1/4 cup of the sugar until the
mixture is thick. Stir in the milk, Straub Beer, and brandy.
Beat the egg whites until foamy. Beat in the remaining
1/4 cup of sugar until stiff peaks form. Fold the egg
whites into the egg yolk mixture. OR, combine the
prepared egg nog, Straub Beer, and brandy, stirring well.

Chill. Before serving, fold in the whipped cream.
Top with more whipped cream and the nutmeg.

Brewing Notes:

YARD OF FLANNEL

Ingredients:

34 ounces Straub Beer
4 eggs
3 tablespoons sugar
1/2 teaspoon ground nutmeg
1/2 teaspoon ground cinnamon
1/2 cup Haitian Rum
Boiling water

Directions:

Heat the Straub Beer in a saucepan over a low heat.
Beat the eggs with the other ingredients and pour the
mixture into a pitcher. Pour the Straub Beer into the egg
mixture, stirring until frothy.

Brewing Notes:

STRAUB'S
STRAWBERRY SLUSH

Ingredients:

1 package Strawberry Kool-Aid
3 cups sugar
6 ounces frozen orange juice
4 1/2 cups warm water
1 (10-ounce) package strawberries
1 cup vodka
1/2 cup Straub Beer
Ginger ale (to taste)

Directions:

Dissolve the Kool-Aid, sugar, and orange juice in the warm water. Add the other ingredients, except the ginger ale, stirring well. Freeze. To serve, scoop the slushy mixture into a glass and add the ginger ale to taste.

Brewing Notes:

MOJO PUNCH

Ingredients:

1 quart light rum
1 quart dark rum
16 ounces cherry brandy
1 quart + 8 ounces Straub Beer
5 cans 7-Up
4 quarts pineapple juice
2 or more bags of ice
Cherries (to float in the punch)

Directions:

Combine all ingredients, stirring well.

Brewing Notes:

"I went on a diet, swore off drinking and heavy eating, and in fourteen days I lost two weeks."

Joe E. Lewis

Straub Beer
Floats & Milkshakes

STRAUB
ROOT BEER FLOAT

Ingredients:

12 ounces Straub Beer
6 tablespoons vanilla ice cream
4 ounces root beer schnapps

Directions:

Combine all ingredients in a blender, blending until
smooth.

Brewing Notes:

STRAUBERRY
FLOAT

Ingredients:

12 ounces Straub Beer
3 scoops strawberry ice cream
Whipped cream
Cherries or strawberries

Directions:

Combine the Straub Beer and ice cream. Garnish with
the whipped cream and cherries or strawberries.

Brewing Notes:

TRIPLE
MINT
FLOAT

Ingredients:

12 ounces Straub Beer
3 scoops mint-chocolate chip ice cream
1 teaspoon crème de menthe
Chocolate mint candy (Andes) (shaved)
Sprig of mint

Directions:

Combine the Straub Beer, ice cream, and crème de
menthe in a blender, blending until smooth. Top with the
chocolate mint candy shavings and garnish with the sprig
of mint.

Brewing Notes:

STRAUB BEER CHOCOLATE MILKSHAKE

Ingredients:

3 ounces Straub Beer
Splash of Jack Daniel's Whiskey
2 cups Kahlua
2 cups milk
1 cup tonic water
1 quart chocolate ice cream

Directions:

Combine all ingredients in a blender, blending until smooth.

Brewing Notes:

STRAUB BEER VANILLA CREAM FLOAT

Ingredients:

1/2 glass Straub Beer
1/2 glass vanilla ice cream
Whipped cream
Small marshmallows
Cherry

Directions:

Pour the Straub Beer over the ice cream. Freeze the mixture for several hours until slushy. To serve, top with the whipped cream, marshmallows, and cherry.

Brewing Notes:

STRAUB'S COCONUT FLOAT

Ingredients:

2 tablespoons coconut rum
1/2 glass Straub Beer
1/2 glass vanilla ice cream
Shredded coconut
Whipped cream
Cherry

Directions:

Pour the rum and then the Straub Beer over the ice cream. Freeze the mixture for several hours until slushy. To serve, top with the shredded coconut, whipped cream, and cherry.

Brewing Notes:

"The man that isn't jolly after drinking is just a driveling idiot, to my thinking."

Euripedes

Straub Beer
On Fire

STRAUB BEER FLAMING DOCTOR PEPPER

Ingredients:

3/4 ounce amaretto
1/4 ounce Bacardi 151 Proof Rum
1/2 cup Straub Beer

Directions:

Combine the amaretto and rum in a shot glass. Pour the
Straub Beer into a tall glass. Light the shot on fire and
drop it into the glass of Straub Beer. Making sure that the
flame is extinguished, chug.

Use extreme caution with the fire.

Brewing Notes:

STRAUB BEER
FLAMEMAKER

Ingredients:

2 ounces Everclear
12 ounces Straub Beer

Directions:

Pour the Everclear into a shot glass and the Straub Beer
into a tall glass. Light the shot on fire and drop it into the
glass. Making sure that the flame is extinguished, chug.

Use extreme caution with the fire.

Brewing Notes:

CRAIG'S
OUTHOUSE SLAMMER

Ingredients:

1 ounce Everclear
3 ounces cola
2 ounces Straub Beer

Directions:

Pour the Everclear into a shot glass. Combine the cola
and Straub Beer in a tall glass, stirring well. Light the
shot on fire and drop it into the glass. Making sure that
the flame is extinguished, chug.

Use extreme caution with the fire.

Brewing Notes:

STRAUB BEER
BARN BURNER

Ingredients:

32 ounces Everclear
6 ounces Straub Beer
16 ounces milk

Directions:

Combine all ingredients in a pitcher, stirring well. Pour
the mixture into tall glasses. Light the mixture on fire.
Once the fire goes out, drink.

Use extreme caution with the fire.

Brewing Notes:

STRAUB BEER
BURNING BUSH

Ingredients:

1 ounce Hot Damn
1/2 glass Straub Beer
1/2 glass apple cider

Directions:

Pour the Hot Damn into a shot glass. Pour the apple
cider and Straub Beer into a tall glass. Light the shot on
fire and drop it into the glass. Making sure that the flame
is extinguished, chug.

Use extreme caution with the fire.

Brewing Notes:

STRAUB BEER
BLAZING COMET

Ingredients:

1/2 ounce amaretto
1/2 ounce whiskey
Dash of Everclear
8 ounces Straub Beer

Directions:

Combine the amaretto and whiskey in a shot glass. Top the shot glass mixture with the Everclear. Pour the Straub Beer into a tall glass. Light the shot on fire and drop it into the glass of Straub Beer. Making sure that the flame is extinguished, chug.

Use extreme caution with the fire.

Brewing Notes:

STRAUB BEER
RASPBERRY BONFIRE

Ingredients:

3/4 ounce Chambord Raspberry Liqueur
1/4 ounce Bacardi 151 Proof Rum
8 ounces Straub Beer

Directions:

Layer the liqueur and rum in a shot glass. Pour the
Straub Beer into a tall glass. Light the shot on fire and
drop it into the glass of Straub Beer. Making sure that the
flame is extinguished, chug.

Use extreme caution with the fire.

Brewing Notes:

STRAUB BEER
COCONUT BONFIRE

Ingredients:

1/2 ounce amaretto
1/2 ounce coconut rum
8 ounces Straub Beer

Directions:

Layer the amaretto and rum in a shot glass. Pour the Straub Beer into a tall glass. Light the shot on fire and drop it into the glass of Straub Beer. Making sure that the flame is extinguished, chug.

Use extreme caution with the fire.

Brewing Notes:

STRAUB BEER
FLAMING SAKE BOMB

Ingredients:

3/4 ounce sake
1/4 ounce Everclear
1/2 ounce Midori
16 ounces Straub Beer

Directions:

Pour the sake into a shot glass and top it with the
Everclear. Combine the Midori and Straub Beer in a tall
glass. Light the shot on fire and drop it into the glass.
Making sure that the flame is extinguished, chug.

Use extreme caution with the fire.

Brewing Notes:

STRAUB BEER
TEQUILA SUNBURN

Ingredients:

1 1/4 ounces tequila
Splash of Bacardi 151 Proof Rum
6 ounces Straub Beer

Directions:

Pour the tequila into a shot glass and top it with the rum.
Pour the Straub Beer into a tall glass. Light the shot on
fire and drop it into the glass of Straub Beer. Making sure
that the flame is extinguished, chug.

Use extreme caution with the fire.

Brewing Notes:

"When I read about the evils of drinking, I gave up reading."

Henny Youngman

Alcohol Glossary & Index

Grand Marnier ~ orange-flavored, cognac-based liqueur, 52
Hot Damn ~ a brand of red cinnamon schnapps, 160
Irish Cream (Baileys Irish Cream) ~ liqueur made from cream, whiskey, and sweetener, 60, 92, 99, 109
Irish Mist ~ honey and orange-flavored liqueur with an Irish whiskey base, 35
Jagermeister ~ bitter herbal-flavored liqueur, 60, 108
Kahlua ~ coffee-flavored liqueur, 15, 16, 52, 76, 107, 151
Lambrusco ~ semi-sweet, dry red wine, 128
Liqueur ~ sweet spirit distilled from herbs, fruits, seeds, and peels

> Almond (see Amaretto)
> Anise (see Absinthe and Galliano)
> Banana, 127
> Cinnamon (see After Shock and Rebel Yell 101)
> Coffee (see Kahlua and Tia Maria)
> Drambuie (sweet) (see Drambuie)
> Herbal (see Cynar and Jagermeister)
> Honey and Orange (see Irish Mist)
> Honeydew (see Midori)
> Irish Cream (see Irish Cream)
> Licorice (see Sambuca)
> Melon (see also Midori), 59, 89
> Mint (see Crème De Menthe)
> Orange (see Curacao, Grand Marnier, and Triple Sec)
> Orange (bitter) (see Amer Picon)
> Peach (see Southern Comfort)
> Raspberry, 6, 162
> Strawberry, 87

Midori ~ honeydew melon-flavored liqueur, 88, 96, 164
Ouzo ~ anise-flavored aperitif or appetizer drink, 28
Pisco ~ brandy made from the Muscatel grape, 64
Rebel Yell 101 ~ double cinnamon spiced liqueur, 85
Rum ~ liquor made from molasses or sugarcane, 21, 34, 45, 52, 66, 121, 123, 127, 132, 133

> Bacardi 151 Black Bat, 13
> Coconut (see also Malibu Rum), 59, 153, 163
> Dark, 27, 28, 33, 83, 145
> Haitian, 143
> Light, 65, 128, 138, 145
> Malibu, 13, 21, 40, 135, 156
> 151 Proof, 10, 43, 90, 106, 131, 156, 162, 165
> Spiced, 43
> White, 8

Sambuca ~ licorice-flavored liqueur, 78
Sake ~ beer made from fermented rice, 86, 164
Schnapps ~ strong, flavored spirit

Drink Index

Straub Beer Apple Tree Cider, 58
Straub Beer Babbler, 112
Straub Beer Barn Burner, 159
Straub Beer Bender, 49
Straub Beer Blazing Comet, 161
Straub Beer Bleeder, 21
Straub Beer Blitz, 93
Straub Beer Boilermaker, 74
Straub Beer Buckshot, 88
Straub Beer Bullet, 15
Straub Beer Burning Bush, 160
Straub Beer Buster, 9
Straub Beer Chocolate Milkshake, 151
Straub Beer Chulitro, 64
Straub Beer Cinner, 42
Straub Beer Citrus Sunsation Punch, 116
Straub Beer Coconut Bonfire, 163
Straub Beer Country Lemonade, 20
Straub Beer Creamy Soda, 63
Straub Beer Crush, 50
Straub Beer Dancin' Momma, 83
Straub Beer Depth Charge, 77
Straub Beer Dew Drop, 28
Straub Beer Dreamsicle, 70
Straub Beer Eeking Monkey, 43
Straub Beer Fire & Ice, 39
Straub Beer Flamemaker, 157
Straub Beer Flaming Doctor Pepper, 156
Straub Beer Flaming Sake Bomb, 164
Straub Beer Gin Blast, 97
Straub Beer Ginger Ale, 24
Straub Beer Ginger Punch, 119
Straub Beer Grand Dame, 52
Straub Beer Grizzly, 34
Straub Beer Gypsy, 60
Straub Beer Hangover, 46
Straub Beer Honey Drop, 101
Straub Beer Hoot & Holler, 107
Straub Beer Hot Ballers, 110
Straub Beer Hot Sake Bomb, 86
Straub Beer Iced Tea, 12
Straub Beer Irish Car Bomb, 92
Straub Beer Jammer, 45
Straub Beer Jungle Juice, 8
Straub Beer Lemon Punch, 123
Straub Beer Lemon Tickler, 30
Straub Beer Lunch Box, 84

Straub Beer Mimosa, 37
Straub Beer Mist, 35
Straub Beer New Year's Punch, 120
Straub Beer Night Crawler, 104
Straub Beer Original Fruit Punch, 127
Straub Beer Over Cherry Rocks, 23
Straub Beer Peachy Punch, 137
Straub Beer Pickled Vodka, 105
Straub Beer Pink Punch Bug, 118
Straub Beer Polka Punch, 136
Straub Beer Power Punch, 140
Straub Beer Raspberry Bonfire, 162
Straub Beer Red-Headed Mary, 18
Straub Beer Red, White, & Blue, 57
Straub Beer Rum in the Dark, 27
Straub Beer Sambuca, 78
Straub Beer Screwdriver, 61
Straub Beer Snakebite, 6
Straub Beer Sour Puss, 51
Straub Beer Southern Jack, 41
Straub Beer Sunrise, 14
Straub Beer-Tang, 117
Straub Beer Tequila Sunburn, 165
Straub Beer Tequila Sunrise, 66
Straub Beer Tongue Tingler, 33
Straub Beer Tropical Nectar, 96
Straub Beer Twist & Shout, 53
Straub Beer Vanilla Cream Float, 152
Straub Beer Volcano, 59
Straub Beer Wedding Punch, 133
Straub Beer Widowmaker, 75
Straub Beertini, 44
Straub Berry Picking Punch, 130
Straub Biere, 68
Straub Blue Moon, 38
Straub Hound Dog, 32
Straub Root Beer Float, 148
Straub Vineyard Punch, 125
Straub's Coconut Float, 153
Straub's Holiday Egg Nog, 142
Straub's Hoola Juice, 11
Straub's Shooting Stars, 108
Straub's Strawberry Slush, 144
Strauberry Daiquiri, 65
Strauberry Float, 149
Strauberry Jolt, 87
Straubuie, 98

About the Author

John E. Schlimm II is the great-great-grandson of Peter and Sabina Straub, founders of the Straub Brewery, Inc. in St. Marys, PA. John is an author, educator, and folk artist. His other books include *The Ultimate Elk Cookbook from the Heart of Elk Country* (with Steven K. Troha), *The Straub Beer Cookbook*, and *Corresponding With History*.

"The horse and mule live thirty years
And never know of wine and beers.
The goat and sheep at twenty die
Without a taste of scotch or rye.
The cow drinks water by the ton
And at eighteen is mostly done.
The dog at fifteen cashes in
Without the aid of rum or gin.
The modest, sober, bone-dry hen
Lays eggs for noggs and dies at ten.
But sinful, ginful, rum-soaked men
Survive three-score years and ten.
And some of us, though mighty few
Stay pickled 'til we're ninety-two."

Charles Duffy